101 Essays to Empower You to Achieve Greatness

Frank Agin
Founder & President
AmSpirit Business Connections

ISBN: 978-1-967521-26-5

Published by:
418 Press, A Division of Four Eighteen Enterprises LLC
Post Office Box 30724, Columbus, Ohio 43230-0724

Acknowledgement

In sincere appreciation of Frances Ann Jackson.

You've empowered a lifetime of success and continual drive.

Table of Contents

Look For These Other Books in This Series

101 Essays to Empower You to Rise & Thrive
101 Essays to Empower You to Up Your Game
101 Essays to Empower You to Build Momentum
101 Essays to Empower You to Limitless Reach
101 Essays to Empower You to Elevate Your Influence
101 Essays to Empower You to Peak Performance
101 Essays to Empower You to The Winning Edge
101 Essays to Empower You to Live Unstoppable
101 Essays to Empower You to Break Barriers

Introduction

This book comes from the insight and creativity of Frank Agin.

Who is Frank? He is the founder and president of AmSpirit Business Connections, an organization that empowers entrepreneurs, sales representatives, and professionals to become successful and gain more referrals through networking.

He is the author of several books, including *Foundational Networking: Building Know, Like and Trust to Create a Lifetime of Extraordinary Success* and *The Three Reasons You Don't Get Referrals*. See all his books and programs at frankagin.com.

Finally, Frank shares information and insights on professional relationships, business networking and best practices for generating referrals on the Networking Rx podcast.

In the summer of 2018, he started planning this short-form podcast. As he mapped out what he wanted to bring to an audience of entrepreneurs, sales representatives, and professionals, he knew he'd have hundreds of programs.

But in addition to all that content, Frank noticed he also had a plethora of other materials—instructive, insightful, and inspirational. All this additional content was worthwhile, but none of it was long enough to create a full episode of Networking Rx.

Not wanting the material to go to waste, Frank developed it into short essays—approximately 150 words each. Then he started to record and share those segments daily under the brand Networking Rx Minutes.

For years, he shared a daily message of empowerment, intuition, and hope. This is a compilation of 100 of those essays. Enjoy.

-1-
Be a Social Catalyst

In chemistry, there is the notion of a catalyst. That's where one substance increases the rate of reaction of another without being consumed itself. For example, when making ammonia, iron is a helpful catalyst. You see, iron accelerates the breaking of nitrogen bonds to make it more reactive to hydrogen. But at the end of the process, the same amount of iron remains.

But catalysts are not limited to chemistry. This same notion can be applied to relationships and networking.

For example, when you introduce two contacts, and one becomes a client of the other. Or when you devote time and energy to uplift a colleague. Or when you inspire an initiative to build financial education in your community. You become the catalyst. You aren't diminished in the least. Nevertheless, it's your activity, energy and presence that increases the rate of reaction.

So, commit to being a social catalyst in your world.

-2-
The Sounding Board

In the legal profession, there is a saying: "An attorney that represents himself has a fool for a client." In short, this implies that the situation impairs the attorney's judgment, preventing them from acknowledging their own shortcomings. They're too close to the situation to see the bigger picture. And they're too emotionally overwhelmed to be objective.

This is simply human psychology. This shortcoming, however, is not limited to the legal profession. It doesn't matter what your professional avocation might be. The advice you give yourself might be the worst you get.

Sure, you know your situation best. That's a given. But how your situation interplays with the bigger picture might not be your forte. Recognize and accept that.

You've worked to create a reliable and trustworthy network. Don't just look to it for referrals and other business opportunities. You should also use it as a sounding board as you embark on new initiatives or face challenging situations. Chances are you'll end up with a better result.

-3-
Happy New Beginnings

Pam Christian, mindset coach and host of *The Juice* podcast shares on her blog, "You know that expression, 'new year, new you'? I don't know about you, but that has always driven me crazy. I kind of feel like using January 1 as a deadline for resetting just sets us up for disappointment and failure."

Christian's point is insightful, and she goes on to say, "New beginnings happen the moment that you decide you want something different for yourself—something better—and then you take steps to make it happen."

She's right. New beginnings happen wherever and whenever you decide. And it doesn't matter if you only take a baby step. And it doesn't matter if a step forward is followed by a step or two back. You just need to take that step to create a new life or new initiative.

So, make the commitment. In this moment, life starts anew. Happy new beginnings.

-4-
The Flexible Mindset

In one of his weekly newsletters, Mark Given, author, speaker, and innovator of the trust-based philosophy, draws a distinction between mental flexibility and an imprisoned mindset. He shares that flexible thinking is your ability to switch your thought process in response to a change in circumstances or an unexpected situation.

The alternative is rigid, mechanical thinking, where you can get locked into a thought process that does not allow you to update or improve what you're telling yourself. This is akin to negative self-talk. "Oh, woe is me … I can't … I'm not good enough."

Given shares that this imprisoned mindset is easy to fall into and a dangerous place to be. And while mental flexibility takes works, it leads to better results.

As Given encourages, "Take a few moments today, then all this week to think about the many things you CAN improve. It's really not that hard to compete and stay ahead of the pack when you think differently and act differently."

-5-
Find Those Who Value You

A father said to his son: "Take this 200-year-old watch my great-grandfather gave me and see what's the best price you can get for it."

The son took the watch to a watchmaker. He, however, only offered five dollars because the piece was old.

The son then went to a jeweler. She, however, only offered twenty-five dollars, as the watch had noticeable wear and scratches.

The son then went to a museum. The curator offered a million dollars for the rare antique.

When the son reported back with these offers, his sage father used them as a teachable moment. He said, "I wanted to let you know that the right place values you in the right way. Find that place."

The father's lesson applies to you. If someone does not value what you have to offer, move on. And don't settle. Find the situation that appropriately values you.

-6-
The 35-Year Swim

In his book *No One Gets There Alone*, leadership and sports psychologist Dr. Rob Bell shares a story about Diana Nyad – the first person to successfully swim from Cuba to the United States.

While the distance between the two countries is only about 110 miles, it took Nyad 35 years to complete the feat. No, the ultra-distance swimmer was not in the water all that time. However, in 1978 she formulated the vision and along the way she endured four failed attempts.

But by 2013, she'd assembled the right team, had the right conditions and the right mindset to overcome the naysayers who proclaimed that "it can't be done."

Big visions are inspiring things. But they just don't manifest themselves. No, of course not. To realize the big vision you have for yourself, you need a network of people to support you. And you need to create the conditions and harness a mindset to see it through.

-7-
Defining Networking

Often people view networking and prospecting as one and the same. Sure, prospecting can be a subset of networking, but it is a very, very narrow one.

Remember, this distinction. Prospecting is nothing more than looking for that next client. And making that sale is nothing more that attempting to taking away someone's pain or providing them pleasure based on the goods or services you offer. Nothing about that is bad, but networking is so much more.

You see, networking is much broader in nature. It's focused on building relationships, learning about others, and finding ways to add value to them that go beyond what you sell.

Sure, building these caring relationships can lead to sales … and it often does. But that's not the primary intent. Networking and building caring relationships is about alleviating pain or bringing pleasure via any means possible.

-8-
Inspiration All Around

Everyone needs it. Everyone needs a little inspiration from time to time. After all, business is hard. Life is hard. Everything is hard. But a little inspiration provides that small boost to keep you going. Inspiration offers hope that you can overcome. And it's clear evidence that success is possible.

This then begs the question: Where do you find inspiration?

Here is the reality: Inspiration is all around you. Inspiration happens everywhere. It happens every day. It might not be something miraculous. It might not be something Herculean in nature. It's likely just someone finding happiness in their everyday life. But if you are looking for inspiration, you can easily find it. You just need to open your heart and mind and believe it's there.

Then once you find it, seize upon it and take it in. And use that moment of inspiration – whether it's big or small – to propel you towards wherever you are headed.

-9-
What's Limiting You?

American self-help guru Tony Robbins once shared:

"Like most of us, you've built at least part of your identity on other people's expectations. The process of internalizing the values of others was unconscious. And bringing it to consciousness is the essence of learning how to become the best version of yourself. By learning to recognize and let go of whatever limiting beliefs are keeping you from self-actualization, you're able to push forward and find the person you really are."

Success is not a destination, some place to arrive. But rather success is continuing to move along a path of improvement and self-discovery.

And that's not always easy. It takes courage to acknowledge all the things you are not. And there are often challenges to becoming the person you could and should be. Overcoming these usually takes persistence.

A key first step is recognizing and letting go of what's holding you back.

-10-
Gaining The Trust of Others

There is a natural order of most things. One being that you do something, and that something creates results. If you want to be physically fit, first you need to put in the effort of exercise and being mindful of what you eat. If you want to take money out of the bank, you first need to put money into the bank.

And this natural order also applies to getting people to trust you. If you are looking to gain the trust of others, the key is to become trusting first.

This does not advocate taking needless financial risks or putting yourself in harm's way. It does, however, suggest that you start by giving others the benefit of the doubt. It continues by believing that others will do the right thing. And it's capped off by interacting with others with the simple understanding that everyone wants to be accepted and respected.

If you want the trust of others, the first move belongs to you.

-11-
Bit By Bit Over Time

Dream big. Set lofty goals. Aspire to massive achievement.

Those all sound great. But when it comes time to get to work, the journey can seem daunting. After all, big, lofty, or massive cannot, by definition, be achieved overnight. Rather, any of these come about over years, if not decades.

Thus, it's only natural that you'll have a sense of frustration from time to time. You know, those moments where you feel exhausted by all the effort you've expended. And yet at the same time, the massive achievement you aspire to still seems a long way off.

When you encounter such moments, reflect on this famous Malay saying: 'sedikit-sedikit, lama-lama jadi bukit." Loosely translated it means "Bit by bit, over time, it will accumulate into a mountain."

No doubt, this fits your situation somehow. Truly lofty goals are simply not achievable overnight. No, those mountains are scaled bit by bit over time.

-12-
Earn Your Way Out

In her book *The Six Habits: Practical Tools For Bringing Your Dreams To Life*, TEDx speaker Laura DiBenedetto shares about her challenging path to success. She writes: "Misery knows no prejudice. You can be a poor and kicked around kid like me, or you can be the rich popular kid that has it all. It doesn't matter because we all have our issues."

This is an insightful point. Everyone faces challenges and misery. They might not be obvious, but they are there. Only you truly know yours. And while you can get help from others to tackle what ails you, you – and only you – can take the necessary action to correct the situation.

As DiBenedetto goes on to share: "You can't buy your way out, you can't drink your way out, you can't exercise your way out, and you can't even think your way out. We all have but one path: do the work and earn the way out."

-13-
Shoulders of Giants

Sir Isaac Newton, 17th century mathematician and astronomer, credited with formulating the laws of motion and universal gravity, once remarked after being lauded for his amazing scientific achievements: "If I have seen further than others, it is by standing upon the shoulders of giants."

Newton coined this metaphor believing that much of the credit for his contribution to the world was because of discoveries that came before him. And this was true. Prior advancements in astronomy, mathematics, and physics provided the foundation upon which his discoveries were based.

But the same is true for you. Chances are, parents or other loved ones ensured that you got up and went to school. Teachers and instructors helped you advance along a curriculum of reading, writing and arithmetic. A professional someone gave you a chance, while others have mentored you. And you're finding success in industries that others created.

Whatever you've accomplished, you stand on the shoulders of giants.

-14-
Reinvention

In his weekly *Reinvented* blog series, John Millen, a professional speaker, transformational leadership trainer and personal developer, related a story of reinvention. In it, he shared how actor Matthew McConaughey went from being one of Hollywood's most sought-after romantic comedy stars to the Academy Award winning Best Actor in 2014 for a role that was anything but rom-com.

McConaughey intentional reinvented himself by turning down multi-million-dollar roles in rom-com movies. As Millen shares, "McConaughey stood his ground and paid a heavy price that proved his commitment." This was a tremendous sacrifice for the actor, as it forced him to downsize his lavish lifestyle that he and his family enjoyed.

If you aren't happy with the direction of your life, change it. It won't be easy, and it will take sacrifice. But you don't have to accept the path you're on.

-15-
The Invisible Machine

Having an incredible network is empowering. It creates a sort of invisible machine that will churn out for you over time lots of referrals, contacts, information, opportunities, and encouragement.

But having an incredible network doesn't just happen. It takes a large degree of intentionality and a huge splash of accountability. That said, you need to start the day by committing to taking action to build the relationships around you. Give referrals. Make introductions. And share information, opportunity, and encouragement.

And then you need to check in with yourself at the day's end with an honest assessment: Did you do what you said you were going to do? In that moment, quickly celebrate the wins. And quietly admonish the failures. And then move to the next day.

Whatever the case, commit to doing something every day to develop your network and then follow through. As every action is a step towards building that invisible machine.

-16-
HATs Off To Bias

In her much-acclaimed TEDx talk, *The Pain, Power and Paradox of Bias*, Sejal Thakkar shared about the challenges she faced as the daughter of Indian immigrants attending high school in a predominantly Italian neighborhood near Chicago. She revealed the bias she endured and made the point that everyone holds bias of one sort or another. It's merely human.

Given that, Thakkar provided an acronym – HAT – designed to empower you to be better able to confront any bias you find yourself having.

The H is for Hold Off: When you find yourself drawing a quick conclusion about someone, stop yourself and look for objective facts.

The A is for Ask Why: As you're holding off, take that time to analyze why you're reaching your immediate conclusion.

And the T is for Take Action: Choose to be aware, accepting and inclusive in how you conduct yourself.

Yes, bias is something humans are born with. But it's not something you have to live with.

-17-
Be Human

On the Networking Rx podcast, entrepreneurial coach Kamalini Roy shared this insight: "No technology can replace what a human heart feels for another human heart." Roy, author of *Create Wealth By Creating High-Performance Teams*, is right.

Sure, computers and technology are capable of much. Computation. Searching. Sorting. And programs and apps exist that allow humans to communicate with hundreds of people in nano seconds. As powerful as computer processing has become, these machines will never successfully mimic the human traits of compassion, love, and empathy.

So, while electronic bits and bytes can efficiently make contact, they are completely ineffective in building relationships. Knowing this, don't rely on technology to connect with the hearts and minds of others.

Rather, take the extra time to craft a personal e-mail, at a bare minimum. Or even goes as far as picking up the telephone, set up a ZOOM call, or arrange a face-to-face meeting. In short, be human.

-18-
Recycle Success

One of the things that successful comedians and professional speakers do is document their material. They outline their program. Map out a flow. And work to appropriately vary content.

In this process, they carefully note the bits that work well and track the parts of the program that seem to fall flat. Not surprisingly, the material that hits they keep in their routine. And the stuff that doesn't they substitute out.

While no one may be paying you to speak or make a crowd laugh, you can benefit from this material tracking process.

If you noticed that your friends or colleagues enjoy one of your stories, keep that on hand for the future. If a way you describe something serves to engage conversation partners, don't re-invent the wheel.

In both of these instances, whatever you've said resonates with one audience – even if it's just an audience of one – chances are that material will work with others. So, recycle that success.

-19-
The Giving Lane

Never forget this notion: Networking is a two-way street. You cannot just focus on receiving. If you do, in time, others will realize that you're selfish. And they will lose all hope that you'll add any value to them ... or anyone at all for that matter.

So, to be truly successful with networking, you need not just drive in the "receiving" lane. Occasionally, you need to change directions and drive in the other lane of networking. In short, you need to give, as well. And not just be enriched.

How? Think about it. What's good for you, is likely good for others too.

You want referrals? Others want them too.

You value insightful information? Others could benefit from it as well.

You want new contacts and useful opportunities? So do the people contributing to you.

Remember, you'll get out of networking what you put into it. So, drive in the giving lane of networking, as often as possible.

-20-
Five Whys

In the 1930s, Sakichi Toyoda, founder of Toyota Industries, developed the 5 Whys technique of problem solving, which is still used today. Through this technique one can determine the root cause of a problem by continuing to ask "why?" Each answer forms the basis of the next question.

For example: Why are you not hitting your goals? Because you're failing to devote the appropriate time to important activities.

Why are you not devoting appropriate time to these activities? Because I'm saddled with too many administrative duties.

Why do you have all those administrative duties? Because I don't delegate.

Why don't you delegate? Because I lack the support staff. Why do you lack support staff? Because I haven't asked for approval to fill the position.

In this example, the root cause for not hitting the goal comes down to a simply request. An easy conversation. Maybe just a quick e-mail.

So, what's a problem you're facing? The simple solution may only be the five "whys" away.

-21-
Genie In a Bottle

In his book *MORE: Word of Mouth Referrals, Lifelong Customers & Raving Fans*, word-of-mouth referral consultant Matt Ward shares: "Who doesn't want a genie in a bottle who can answer all their questions and grant all their wishes?"

Ward goes on to share that you have such a genie at your fingertips: The Internet. Via the wonder of the world wide web, you have answers to all your questions. Moreover, as Ward shares, you have the answers to all the questions that those in your network have.

So, take the initiative to find information for your prospects, clients and even centers of influence. In so doing you set yourself apart in their minds and their hearts. They will be completely wowed by your efforts. And as Ward shares, "You will remain on the top of their mind as a resource to tap when they need your products or service."

And that is where the genie in a bottle starts to grant your wishes.

-22-
The 10-Year Test

Life is not easy. It involves lots of hard work. You must deal with challenges and even setback. And mostly, there are decisions that need to be made. Seemingly every day you have dozens of choices to contend with. Often, they are small and inconsequential. From time to time, the decision before you, however, involves choosing between an opportunity or continuing on the path you're taking.

When in such a dilemma, consider the advice that author Marie Forleo shared in the December 2019 issue of Success Magazine. She said, "Imagine yourself 10 years older. Now, ask yourself would I regret not doing something new? In other words, if you don't take on the new endeavor, might you regret it in 10 years? If so, change."

Chances are, moving on will work out. Moreover, there is a reason as to why the opportunity is before you in the first place.

-23-
Punch Holes In The Sky

Mark Given, author, speaker, and innovator of the trust-based philosophy, shared on one of his weekly newsletters that test pilots have a phrase they use to describe their climb to heights and speeds only dreamed of by others. They call it *"punching holes in the sky."*

Given then brings the reader back down to earth reminding them that too many people settle with 'good enough.' They aim for far less than their potential. In time, they convince themselves that their dreams are impossible. Shortly thereafter, they stop trying. And often, this happens just before impossible becomes possible.

He goes on to share: "Truth is, the only real failure in life is the failure to try." He's right. If you really try, there is a chance. And from there, if you expect success, you're much more likely to get it.

So, with whatever you dream, strap yourself in, pull back the throttle, and punch holes in the sky.

-24-
Listen, Summarize, Show

Effective listening skills are not important to communication. No, they're imperative. After all, no one is going to commit energy to what you have to say unless you do the same.

That said, effective listening is not easy. Every second your brain is taking in 11 million bits of information. So, your thoughts cannot help but race. Even as you try to concentrate on the words coming out of your conversation partner's mouth, you mind has trouble focusing.

To manage this process better, try this trick: As you listen, do so with the intention of summarizing the other person's point of view. Then, to show that you were listening, formulate one or two questions that invite the person to clarify. Something like, "When you say your family moved around, how many different states did you live in?"

With repetition, the practice of listen-summarize-show will serve you well.

-25-
The Power of I'm Sorry

You're not perfect. No one is. You're going to make mistakes. Some are simply unintentional. Likely, the product of a bad decision or inexperience. Some might be intentional, saying the wrong thing at the wrong time in a weak moment.

While you generally can't undo a mistake, you can do your best to atone for it. You know, making restitution of some sort and pledging to try not to do it again. But this all starts with a statement of apology.

Whether expressed verbally or in writing, saying "I'm sorry" is a powerful thing. It communicates to another that you've harmed them. Additionally, in that moment you convey a sense of regret. While that might not undo the damage, it serves to disarm anger another may feel towards you.

Again, no one is perfect. But you can move yourself one step closer by making the word "sorry" part of your relationship-building vocabulary.

-26-
Two Sides of Same Coin

In his book, *All You Have To Do Is Ask*, American sociologist and social capital researcher Dr. Wayne Baker shares that asking and giving are different sides of the same coin.

Baker goes on to explain that adding value to your networking is an important first step to building great relationships and centers of influence in your life. But, in time if all you do is give, eventually others become uncomfortable with the arrangement.

Remember, humans are hard wired to reciprocate. In short, they want to help you too. So, the flip side of adding value to others is asking for things in return. Your network needs referrals. You do too. So, ask. The people around you need to be introduced to wonderful centers of influences. You're no different. Remember to ask. You bless others with great opportunities. It would be great to have them too. Again, all you have to do is ask.

-27-
Sailing By Ash Breeze

Mark Given founder of the trust-based philosophy shared in one of his weekly newsletters that, "In the days when sailors depended on wind to carry them to their destinations, it was not uncommon to hear that a ship might be "sailing by ash breeze". The phrase referred to the wind dying out leaving the sailors to row toward their destination, as the oars were made of ash wood."

Why not wait for the wind to return? Given went on to explain that "they were eager to experience what waited for them on land."

Today's existence is similar. At times, your life moves along smoothly. Your career, business, and relationships seem to flow as if a wind were at your back. Other times, however, that momentum is not there.

In these moments, to keep moving forward it takes effort. You need to pull out your metaphorical oars and create your own ash breeze.

-28-
Reach Out and Touch Someone

The civilized world is held together by invisible bonds between humans. These are generally referred to as relationships. And these relationships start and then flourish through communication.

Certainly, humans communicate in lots of ways. What you say. How you say it. Your body language. And how your actions lined up with all of that. Beyond that, however, communication also involves actual contact. It's true. Physical touch is a powerful form of communication.

And the physical touch doesn't need to be overly complicated. Shake someone's hand. Give someone a pat on the shoulder. Be bold and go in for a full-on hug. Or even just offer up a high five or fist bump.

Done appropriately – which certainly varies from situation to situation – physical touch with someone will leave them feeling a stronger sense of rapport with you almost immediately. So, know your audience, and the reach out and touch someone.

-29-
Permission To Be Wrong

In an interview on the full Networking Rx podcast, human-centered coach and consultant Susan K. Lambert offered some advice that a friend once gave her: "Give people permission to be wrong about you."

In essence what Lambert shared is that most everybody does the best that they can do. You try to do the right things. You try to say the right things. You try to interact with others appropriately. Right?

Here's the reality, however. From time to time, you might mess up. That one transgression should not forever cast you as bad person. And from time to time, others might get the wrong impression about you and your good intentions simply because they saw a small glimpse of who you are in the wrong way.

In these moments, people might draw an erroneous conclusion about you. That's okay. There mistake doesn't change you. So, gracefully give them permission to be wrong about you.

-30-
Perfectly Them

Citing findings reported by the National Academy of Sciences, Wharton School of Business professor Dr. Adam Grant said on Twitter:

"Great mentors don't push us to follow in their footsteps. They guide us to blaze our own trail. When mentors let scientists pick their own topics and work independently, they're more likely to become stars. The goal is to help them create and convey their ideas, not clone ours."

Guiding others in not limited to the scientific community. It's part of the human experience. It's safe to say that everyone mentors somebody. A younger employee. A budding entrepreneur. Even, a young child.

As Grant shares, your path is likely not someone else's. But your experiences … your insight … your wisdom can help them down the path they've chosen for themselves. Share those things. Help others succeed on their terms. Remember, you're perfectly you. Let them be perfectly them.

-31-
Making Salt

In Business Secrets of the Bible, author Rabbi Daniel Lapin shares that the chemical compounds Sodium and Chlorine separately are toxic and deadly. Together, however, they become Sodium Chloride, which is commonly known as salt – a wonderful addition to many foods and necessary to sustain life.

Certainly, you aren't deadly or toxic. No one is. Together, with others, however, you are so much more than you are on your own.

The people around you motivate you to do more. And that added effort inspires them to do the same. The people around you are a source of information, ideas, and insights. And in return, you offer the same to them. The people around you help complete you, making you kinder, gentler, and simply a better version of yourself. And that reflects on their presence too.

You need others in your life. It's like you come together and make salt.

-32-
Better Than Better

On the Networking Rx podcast, Jean MacDonald, author of *Finding The Fortune: How to Strengthen Your Follow-Up Strategies and Close More Sales* made this statement: "Different is better than better."

As part of that comment, she shared a story from her book when she was only 10. At the time, all the neighborhood kids were selling lemonade. MacDonald wanted to be part of the action. However, her parents made the point that also selling lemonade was not the key to success – even if it was better than everyone else's. Rather, the key to success was selling something different.

With that, and help from her parents, MacDonald came up with the plan to go door to door taking orders for fresh and canned vegetables. While the other kids made mere pennies hawking lemonade, she made dollar after dollar after dollar doing something complete different.

Just don't be better. Be different. In product. In approach. In service. It'll be more profitable.

-33-
Pig-Headed Discipline

Dan LeFave, business strategist, elite coach and author of the book *"Living the Life of Your Dreams – How To Stop Working Insane Hours And Start Living An Awesome Life"*, shares that one of the keys to success is simply having P.H.D.

No, LeFave is not suggesting that you need to achieve a doctorate from an institution of higher learning, such as Oxford, Harvard, or Yale. What he means is that success is driven by pig-headed discipline, or P.H.D. Sure, devoting a little time to honing your craft is commendable. However, that does not manifest itself into true success until you habitually do it.

So, if you want to separate yourself from a pack of competitors in any industry or profession, figure out what little thing can serve to improve you. That execute on that today. And tomorrow. And day after day, week after week, after that for years on end. Eventually, you'll find yourself on top.

-34-
Focus On Your Rich Life

Imagine this: You have $86,400. That's a vast sum of money. Then one day someone steals ten of those dollars from you. Would you walk away from the remainder of your wealth for a mere handful of money? Of course, not. That would be foolish.

Following similar logic, if someone injects 10 seconds of negativity in your life – however that might manifest itself – don't spend the other 86,390 seconds of the day fretting over it.

From time to time, others have bad moments in their life. And there are simply people around you who have a bad attitude about life. Moreover, from time to time those moments and those people will spill over into your world. You can't control that.

But what you can control is how you react to these mere blips in your day. Accept that these moments are going to happen. And when they do, pledge to move on from them. And focus on the rich life you have.

-35-
Networking – Alive and Well

A couple hundred-thousand years ago, early *man* evolved enough to descend from the trees, walk upright and venture forth. Then in a mere tick of the geological clock, humans had literally populated every nook and cranny of planet Earth.

How did this occur? Humans discovered that they not only improved their chances of survival, but they also increased their level of prosperity, by simply sharing labor, tools, and information. This is networking in its earliest form.

And every step of the way, these forged relationships have guided the human race. And while technology is advancing daily – allowing society to more transient and far-flung – don't bet on the demise of networking.

Working together will always be part of the human experience. Moreover, it will continue to be the primary driver of success and advancement. Networking. It is alive and well.

-36-
Ask Follow-Up Questions

In 2017, an interesting study appeared in the Journal of Personality and Social Psychology. Based on work done at Harvard University, researchers found that men and women who participated in a speed dating exercise could successfully land more dates with suitable partners by doing one simple thing. Ask a follow-up question.

While you might not be looking to secure one more candle-lit dinner, this practice can also be fruitful in your professional world.

If you want to have a successful small talk encounter, you need to get the other person talking. The key to doing this is asking questions. You up the ante on that process, however, by following up on your questions with another.

So, go ahead. Ask someone how they got started in their career. And once they've shared, ask how they knew that things were going to work out for them. This will lead to more appointments ... more introductions ... and, more overall success.

-37-
Get Into the Action

If you went to a networking event, grabbed a chair, and sat along the wall, what would you expect to gain from the experience? Answer: NOTHING!!! To make the event work for you, you need to get up and interact with people.

Social media is much the same. You can expect nothing from it unless you put something into it. You need to make active use of it.

Just like when you head to the networking event, you need to not only be visible, but you need to put your best foot forward. Start with a compelling and unique profile. And then from there, commit to making insightful and value-loaded posts. Don't stop with sharing value, but also engage by liking, commenting, and sharing what others post.

Just like being at an event, show up with your best self and get into the action by communicating with others.

-38-
Ask

In 1972, New York University researcher Thomas Moriarty conducted a social behavior experiment, known as *The Beach Blanket* study. A member of his team would leave his radio on his beach blanket unattended. Then, a few minutes later, another member attempted to steal the radio. Only 20 percent of the time did someone intervene.

Then Moriarty made a simple adjustment to the study. And with that, 95 percent of the time someone intervened and prevented the thief. What was the change? The owner of the radio directly asked his neighbor to keep an eye on his stuff while he had to step away.

As Crystal Dwyer Hansen shares in her book, *Ask: The Bridge From Your Dreams To Your Destiny*, "Human beings are wired to want to help, but they don't. They don't always feel comfortable doing so. They simply don't want to overstep their bounds. So, if you want the help that others are so willing to give, you need to just ask."

-39-
Win With Character

In 2009, Covenant School, a Texas high school girls' basketball team defeated the Dallas Academy in embarrassing fashion – 100 to nothing. In so doing, they provided a clear example that sportsmanship is about more than just losing with grace.

Life is competition. And even though you might not be tallying baskets, goals, or points in your world, you via against others for promotions, great clients or to have the nicest lawn.

And while besting the competition might be the objective, you should never lose sight of the fact opposite you, is another human being. Someone with feelings. Someone who needs to carry on in defeat.

Know this, winning, however it manifests itself, should never be about demoralizing another. It should be about being proud of yourself. But not just proud of what you've done, but also proud as to how you did it. Remember, be of the same character in victory as in defeat.

-40-
Do Good

Sixteenth century prominent English religious figure, John Wesley, wrote:

Do all the good you can,
In all the ways you can,
In all the places you can,
At all the times you can,
To all the people you can,
As long as ever you can...

Look around. There is no shortage of need in the world. Some of it is requiring big effort. Some of it small. And lots more in between. Whatever the case, there is an abundance of opportunity for you to do good.

Sure, your talents and skills lend themselves better to certain situations. No matter. Share them there. Wherever. However. Whenever. To whomever. As long as you can. Bless the world with what you have to offer. Do Good.

-41-
First, Best, Different

Generally, in business, brand success relies on being first, best, or different. As an individual in the working world or out in the community in general, the same rules apply to you. After all, your existence has a brand to it, right?

Following that logic, to stand out from the crowd and be noticed, you need to be first, best, or different. Chances are – unless you've done something remarkable or cutting-edge – you're not first relative to anything.

As for being best, do you really feel comfortable planting your flag on that assertion? After all, who's to say what's best? And, no, dear old mom does not count.

But you can be different. You can be that rare combination of having a strong, positive presence no matter the situation ... being generous with your time, treasure, and talent ... as well as have an unquestioned reliability and integrity.

Yep. Be different. Hitch your brand to that.

-42-
One Single Thought

The human brain is an amazing thing. This three-pound mass of gray matter has more than 100 billion nerves that communicate via trillions of connections. And it all housed in the six inches between your ears.

It coordinates hundreds of body parts into an efficient machine. And it processes millions of pieces of information every moment of your life. And it can hold a lifetime of wonderful memories.

Despite the astonishing abilities of your brain, it has one limitation. Your brain can only allow you one conscious thought at a time. It's true. If you stop and think about dealing with that cantankerous colleague, you cannot be thinking about serving that wonderful client you're about to land.

Knowing this, you can empower a great disposition simply displacing any negative thoughts you might have with positive, optimistic ones. Simply keep pondering about the potentially wonderful things ahead. And then great thoughts will dominant your mind.

-43-
The Slowest Runner In America

Ben Comen was a remarkable member of South Carolina's L.T. Hanna High School's cross country team. No, he never broke any records. And, no he never won any titles. He wasn't even known for speed. Rather, on any give race day, he was without question the slowest runner on the course.

You see, Comen was notable because of his persistence. Having cerebral palsy, running was difficult. No matter how many times he fell or no matter how hard he fell, he always got back up. No matter how far behind he was from the other runners, he never gave up and always tried to do his best.

And it was that trait – that stick-to-it-ness – that won him the admiration of his teammates, fans, and even opponents. While you might not have such an affliction, you can exercise similar determination. Remember, you don't have to be the best. You just need to try your best.

-44-
Create Game Plans For Success

One of things that everybody on the planet has in common are setbacks. You might not want to admit them. And many people don't. But no one's life is an endless progression of forward progress. And no one perfectly executes on everything that try (even though for some it seems like it).

Certainly, some of these disappointments are small. And it takes little to recover from them. Others are downright tragic. Those might significantly alter your intended path. And then there are various of setbacks in between.

Each of these might leave you feeling a sense of loss. But each of these also provides you with a lesson. Something to grow from. Use these to your advantage.

But more importantly, share them. Whatever you've learned from life's obstacles, could help another avoid them. In a sense, these less-than-stellar moments become game plans for success to someone else.

-45-
Relationships Bring Business

Rooted in the debates of ancient Grecian philosophers arguing about cause and effect, the age-old query is, what came first the chicken or the egg? And that paradox is used metaphorically for lots of situations.

One being this: Does business drive relationships? Or do relationships create business? According to Bridget Hom the answer is clear. The mindset and strategy coach at Bridge to Freedom Coaching shares this mantra with her clients, "Take the business out of your relationships, and your relationships will bring you business."

Hom's words are insightful. Absent some extraordinary circumstances, people do business with those that they know, like, and trust. And that trifecta of qualifiers can only be achieved through a genuine relationship.

Sure, that can serve to impair the notion of quick sales and crushing unrealistic quotas. But what it does create is a foundation for lucrative, long-term business. So, there is no lasting debate about it: Relationships bring business.

-46-
Associate With Balcony Person

In his book *No One Gets There Alone*, sports psychologist and mental health expert Dr. Rob Bell draws a distinction between two types of people: Balcony people and basement dwellers.

Bell shares that basement dwellers are those toxic people who drag you down. They do all they can to undermine you. They discourage good habits. They rail against discipline and goals. And they scoff at anything that could serve to advance you.

Conversely, balcony people work to lift you up. They have qualities you aspire to. Moreover, they encourage and challenge you attain them. And they are happy even if you surpass them. And when see you're struggling with something, they work to help guide you forward.

In reality, both basement dwellers and balcony people want you to be at their level. One seeks to pull you down. The other lift you up. Where do you want to be? No brainer, huh? Associate with balcony people.

-47-
Give Me A Report

The business world and your personal life are stitched together by relationships. These are real connections with others – family, friends, colleagues, and acquaintances. With these people you develop a mutual sense of knowing, liking, and trusting.

The building blocks of these three elements are forged in many ways. One is by simply having conversations. Now, some of these are meaningful exchanges. And others are seemingly idle banter. Whatever the case, the most important part of this dialogue is where you just listen – taking in what the other person is saying.

An effective listening skill is to adopt the mindset that when you listen to another you have the obligation of giving a third person a report on the conversation later.

This tactic forces you to concentrate. It helps you remember. And mostly, it serves to build better relationships.

-48-
You Let Me Down

On Twitter, Wharton School professor Dr. Adam Grant shares that: "When people let you down, you owe it to them to let them know. Hiding disappointment breeds resentment—and sets them up to keep disappointing you. Explaining how their actions fell short of your expectations isn't unkind. It's an investment in improving the relationship."

Grant is right. Your life is wrapped up with the people around you. To the extent you can help them improve and become the best version of themselves, it only serves to raise you up too.

Nothing herein suggests that you should become preachy or meanspirited. Rather this conversation is an opportunity for you to demonstrate that you care about them. Moreover, you care about your ongoing relationship with them. And that the purpose in sharing about how you felt let down will lead to a brighter tomorrow for both of you.

-49-
Failure Equals Feedback

In his book *The School of Greatness*, lifestyle entrepreneur and high-performance business coach Lewis Howes shares: "In reality failure is feedback. It's not that you're bad or not good enough or incapable. Failure gives you the opportunity to look at what's not working and figure out how to make it work."

As he implies, embrace failure. As much as those moments can hurt, with the appropriate mindset they can lead to a sense of elation. Yes, elation! After all, there are only so many potential paths to success. Failure simply alerts you to routes that are not successful.

As Howes continues, "Thomas Edison endured 10,000 failures before he made the lightbulb. But each 'failure' was feedback telling him that he hadn't figured it out yet." But with the knowledge from each setback, it increased Edison's likelihood of success on the next attempt.

So, failure is not really a setback. Rather, it's gathering feedback.

-50-
The Golden Guideline

The golden rule of networking is simply "give first, get second." Translated, this means that before you should expect anything from those around you, you need to give to your network first. Introductions. Information. Encouragement. Support. Referrals and opportunities.

Once you've added this value, you'll have set in motion powerful psychological forces that inspire others to do similar things for you. While this notion generally holds true, it's possible that you find yourself feeling like you've received before you've done anything at all. How could this be?

Consider this, the golden rule of networking is more a guideline than an ironclad rule. And there are wonderful people out there looking to contribute to the lives of others. And you might just be graced by someone's noble gesture.

Should this happen, consider yourself blessed. Then set about either returning their deed or paying it forward by helping another. In the end, it will all even out.

-51-
You Are What You Do

Tell the world you're hard working. It's meaningless. Share out that you're honest. So what? Continue to remark that you're disciplined and resilient. It doesn't indicate that you are.

Here is the reality: What you post or profess about yourself carries very little weight. Rather, it's what you do that matters most.

If you want to be known as hard working, then lean your shoulder into whatever you do. You never need to share that you're honest. Just relentlessly be that person. And you never need to remark about your discipline and resilience if you simply conduct yourself as such.

The persona you hope to be known for never comes from self-proclamation. It comes from tireless action and setting an unrelenting example. You are not what you say. Rather, you are what you do.

-52-
Just Be Yourself

The reality is that no matter who you are and no matter what you do, not everyone is going to like you.

Certainly, you can endeavor to transform yourself. However, at the same time this transformation will likely alienate the affection of those who liked you just the way you are. There is nothing you can do. Not everyone is going to like you. You need simply need to stop trying to make it happen.

Remember, there are seven billion people on this rock called Earth. Amongst this mass of humanity, there are more than enough people who will accept you just the way you are.

Certainly, be respectful of others and who they are. But for you, simply endeavor to be yourself. After all, it's what you are best at doing.

-53-
Cable News Networking

The best time to start building relationships is long before you need them.

As an example, consider the case of the Cable News Network, better known as CNN. In January 1991, the Persian Gulf War began with a massive U.S.-led air offensive known as Operation Desert Storm. As it did, the Iraqi government sought to black out media coverage by ejecting all foreign reporters.

This was largely successful, as all major media outlets were ousted. However, the upstart CNN was able to keep its correspondents in place. But how?

It was not luck. Nor an oversight. Rather, it was the relationships that CNN founder, Ted Turner, had forged well before the Gulf War began. You see, for years Turner invited Middle Eastern news affiliates to the U.S. to attend seminars. The contacts hid the CNN staff and allowed them to keep reporting as the war waged on.

Build relationships today. Benefit from them one day.

-54-
The Hedonic Treadmill

Imagine this: A long, lost uncle leaves you gobs of money. Now you're wealthy. You'd be jumping for joy. But in time, your level of happiness would come back down to about where it's at now.

Now, imagine this: You're in a horrible car accident. You survive, but it leaves you wheel car bound for the rest of your life. You'd be sad. But in time, your level of happiness would spring back to where it is now.

These are realities of human psychology. It's called Hedonic adaptation. And studies have shown that humans to quickly return to a relatively stable level of happiness despite major recent positive or negative life events.

So, your happiness does not hinge on good luck, awful circumstances, or any situation. No, your happiness depends solely on your attitude. Whoever you are. Whatever you've achieved. Be grateful for it. Be ecstatic about it. That will lead you to happiness.

-55-
Strive For Average

Most people aspire to be amazing. They long to stand out in the crowd. Be iconic. They want others look up at them in awe. Do you know what's better than be amazing? Simply this: Being average.

This is not to suggest that you settle for mediocrity. Don't do that. You should work hard, become disciplined, and endeavor to achieve. But as you do, reach out and help others do the same. Essentially, as you ascend in life, bring others with you.

Sure, by doing this you might give up the chance to be that someone others look up at in amazement. But what you get in return is to be surrounded by accomplished people who truly care about you for assisting them. And you build into your world a great network of others who cannot wait for the opportunity to help raise you up too.

So don't settle for amazing. Rather strive for average.

-56-
Not Okay To Quit

Deborah Coviello, author of *The CEO's Compass* and host of The Drop-In CEO podcast, shares, "So far, you have overcome every obstacle that you've encountered. It's okay to be tired. It's okay to feel heavy. It's okay to ask for help. It's not okay to quit."

As someone with over 25 years of high-level corporate experience, Coviello knows firsthand that climbing the ladder is hard. Likewise, business is hard. Raising a family is hard. Maintaining relationships is hard. Each of these things can leave you, at times, feeling tired and heavy.

In fact, the only thing about life that is easy is quitting. But as Coviello implies that is not the path to anything. Sure, you can take a pause to gather yourself. And you are well advised to reach out to seek assistance from others. But it's never okay to metaphorically raise a white flag and surrender.

-57-
Spend, Save, Share

Work hard. Be a good person. Things will come your way. And when it does money will likely be part of that equation. Whatever that windfall, to ensure balance in your life, do these three things.

One, spend some. No doubt, you've toiled and sacrificed. You deserve a little something. A nice meal. A gadget. Maybe a trip. Whatever, have some fun.

Two, save some. There is never a guarantee that good times will continue. And one day, you'll want to slow down a bit. So, putting some of your payout aside. That will help prepare for unfortune setbacks and eventual retirement.

Finally, share some. There are people out there with less than you and there are organization who serve them. Use a bit of what you have to ease those burdens.

Following this "spend some, save some, share some" mantra will keep you happy, financially secure, and in good favor with the world.

-58-
Antidote To Loss

Renowned author and leadership guru John C. Maxwell says, "When we are winning nothing hurts; when we are losing everything hurts." This statement is so true. When things are going well you tend to overlook so much.

But when you've experienced a setback every annoyance in your life is magnified. And you tend to become irritable at the smallest of things. And that doesn't reflect well on who you are.

While "everything might hurt in these moments," you're in control of what you present to the world. Sure, it is only natural to experience a certain degree of disappointment that accompanies any failures.

But gather yourself. Work through the pain. Take stock of all the wonderful things you have in your life. Learn from the situation. Then stand tall. Now, move forward working towards your next win. That's the antidote to most any loss.

-59-
Learning From Stonehenge

Stonehenge is perhaps the world's most famous prehistoric monument. Built over 5,000 years ago, near what is now London, this is a unique circle of rectangular stones standing upright.

How it was built is not really known, as somehow these two-ton stones were lifted into place long before any modern machinery.

One theory as to how Stonehenge rocks were stood up into place was using a simple wooden wedge. With that, one could get a stone a sixteenth of an inch off the ground. Then an eighth. Then an inch. Then a foot. Then feet off the ground. Then upright. It's entirely plausible.

So, what's that metaphorical thin edge of the wedge you can use to get you started on accomplishing something big in your life? Use that to get a foothold. Then slowly build from there. Tiny opportunities grow and grow into monumental things.

-60-
Fan The Flames

The lesson is simple: When things are moving in the right direction and a positive outcome is inevitable, it is a natural tendency to sit back and relax. This is the time, however, when you can realize an extraordinary return just by leaning in a little bit more.

When things are going well, you need to challenge yourself to get out to one more event, make one more call or delve a little deeper into social media. These small extra efforts will yield relatively substantial returns for you, simply because you already have the momentum.

As metaphor, consider this: If you set a match to a pile of sticks, there is a strong possibility that the fire may burn itself out before it has an opportunity to spread. If you gently fan the flames, however, you can quickly transform a single match into a raging fire.

-61-
Appear Superhuman

Mark Given, author, speaker, and innovator of the trust-based method, shared in his weekly newsletter: "To make mistakes is human. To own your mistakes is divine!"

He continues with, "Nothing elevates a person higher than to quickly admit and take personal responsibility for the mistakes they make. And you can elevate yourself even higher by fixing your mistake fairly. When you mess up...fess up!"

Given goes on to imply that taking ownership for your shortcomings – no matter how small – actually changes how people feel about you. They come to know you better. They cannot help but like more. And it serves to build their trust in you.

Given wraps up his short piece remarking, "We're all human, so when you screw it up ... own it, embrace it, and lean into it. In today's world...that powerful habit can make you appear superhuman."

-62-
Just Get On Base

According to Major League Baseball, home runs are responsible for a low percentage of runs scored. Rather, the vast majority of runs are the result of just getting on base. Sure, there is an incredible excitement to the sound of the ball cracking off a bat and sailing over the wall hundreds of feet away.

But over time, it's plain old hits or walks that prove to be the most productive. Think about it. It's these ho-hum events in baseball that create potential. But swinging for the fences is an all or nothing proposition.

The same is true of networking. Most of the productivity is not the result of home run contacts. Rather, most of what you accomplish is a result of what you do with all the relatively small individual contacts you make.

So, when you head out to network today (or any day), don't worry about going long. Just get on base.

-63-
Conversation Flint

When you meet new people, it's imperative that you build relationships. This starts by engaging them in a small talk conversation, which is nothing more than getting the other person talking.

This might seem easier said than done. However, here is a simple trick to make it happen. When you receive somebody else's business card, don't put it away immediately.

Rather, keep it in your hand for a while. Look at it. What do you see? Perhaps an area code that suggests that they are from somewhere else. A unique spelling to their name. Their title. A business name. A tagline. A background image. Any of it ... actually, all of it is fodder for creating conversation.

So, using something on the card, ask a meaningful, open-ended question. Then listen. Take an interest. Be curious. This will naturally spark another question. And then another. So, that business card is like a flint to spark the flame of conversation.

-64-
Go Ahead and Suck

On the full Networking Rx podcast, speaker, trainer, and executive coach John Nimmo shared that, "You have to be willing to suck at something to become good at something."

The author of *Why Wait? A Leader's Perspective on Procrastination* went on to share that whenever you started something new you really aren't very good at it. But it's through continued practice and experience you got better and better.

Nimmo is right. Think about it. Tying your shoe? When you embarked on this skill you were all thumbs. Now, it's an unconscious endeavor. Riding a bike? When you started you needed extra wheels, right? Now, you literally cannot forget how to do it.

Pick anything you're good at. It didn't start that way. It never does. So, when you embark onto something new, and it generally doesn't begin so well, do not despair. It's supposed to be like that. Keep after it. Never be afraid to suck at something new.

-65-
Sharpen Your Ax

Abraham Lincoln, the 16th President of the United States once remarked, "If I have nine hours to cut down a tree, I'm going to spend the first six sharpening my ax."

Apply similar logic to your networking endeavors. Before you pick up the phone ... before you launch that video conference ... before you walk into that event ... take the time to plan.

Organize your thoughts. Define your purpose. Envision the results that you'd like to achieve. Get a sense as to who might be there or who'll be talking to. Conduct a little research via LinkedIn. Or perhaps a simple search of the Internet to give you some information or intel on those you'll meet.

Like sharpening an ax, this investment of time will serve to make your networking efforts more efficient. And it will likely make the relationships you build more fruitful.

-66-
The Great Irony

In 1790, George Washington referred to our young country as the "great experiment for promoting human happiness." And, well, by its very nature experiments have flaws. So, America, as we know her, is not perfect. She's a wonderful work in progress.

And, over the years in these United States of America, there are those who have taken it upon themselves to rail on these imperfections. Fair enough. It's the American way to speak out against wrongs and injustices.

Some speak through action. They'll protest at governmental buildings. They'll burn the flag. They'll take a knee during the Star Spangled Banner.

And while these actions might serve to anger you, these acts are really a great irony. You see by being allowed to burn or knee at the very symbol that represents those who fought and died to make this country great, these activists actually serve to show how great this country is.

-67-
The Refillable Glass

People speak about perspective in terms of a glass of water. Those who are optimistic are said to see it as half full. And those who are pessimistic see it as half empty.

And while those perspectives are clear. Neither, however, underscores the most important point. The reality is that no matter how you find or see your world at any given moment, you can change the situation.

That is, when life seems to be trending in an undesirable direction, you can make efforts to change it. Even when things are going well and momentum is in your favor, you can lean in and make things even better.

At times, the glass just might feel half empty. And in other moments, you might perceive your glass to be half full. But no matter what, your glass is definitely refillable.

-68-
Share the Credit

You're accomplished. You've achieved. You've succeeded. And you've attained. Your life is full of wonderful milestones. And you should be proud of every one of them, as each took hard work and discipline. While you are due kudos and a hardy pat on the back, know this: With any triumph in your life some credit is due others too.

No matter what you've done, and no matter how you did it, you've done nothing alone. Behind you ... alongside of you ... or, in front of you were others. They shared encouragement, support, and advice. They may have made an important introduction. Perhaps, they opened your eyes to an opportunity. Maybe they worked alongside of you.

Whatever the case, it wasn't just you. So, share the credit. Thank others for their contribution. Acknowledge their efforts. Shine the light on them. You will end up with more in the end.

-69-
Decision Fatigue

Social psychologist Roy F. Baumeister, known for his work on subjects related to discipline and self-control, shared that humans only have a finite amount of mental energy to expend each day. And like a muscle, these energies are depleted by every decision.

For example, you ponder over whether to respond to e-mails or check social media. And if you decide to check e-mails, you need to determine how you'll prioritize whom you respond to. And if once you you've settled upon who to address first, you pour over every word in your response. It can be exhausting. Moreover, this decision fatigue can impair your ability to effectively interact with others.

Now, you can't avoid all of life's decision. And you cannot change the fact that they deplete your mental abilities. But you can ensure that you have sufficient energies for important relationships by using routines to negate the need for certain decisions as well as planning to have critical interactions with others for during higher energy parts of the day.

-70-
A Mighty Oak

When he was the President of Hiram College, and addressing the notion as to why college takes four years, the United States' 20th President James Garfield once said "When God creates a mighty oak, he takes 100 years. When He looks to make a puny pumpkin, he takes three months."

With that thought, if the accomplishments and achievements you seek are small and insignificant, it's okay to be impatient. You can expect results right now. And you can be frustrated when you don't get them.

But if you're looking to create a mighty oak, so to speak, prepare for the long haul. Some days you will feel as if you're making progress. And other days you will feel as if you are giving ground back. And while you don't have 100 years to see it through, know that it's going to take you more than just three months to achieve the success you seek.

-71-
Humor Up the Hierarchy

A study reported in the 2016 *Journal of Personality and Social Psychology* revealed that an indicator of one's position in the social hierarchy is their ability to utilize humor. Based on the work of researchers from the Harvard and the Wharton Schools of Business, funny people are seen as having a higher status than people who carry themselves in a stoic fashion.

No doubt, humor can be risky. That is something that the researchers acknowledge, as well. But like business ventures or investments, playing it safe seldom yields remarkable rewards.

Moreover, while humor can be risky, that doesn't mean that all humor is offensive. Cute one-liners. Self-depreciating comments. Plays on words. Remarks about the weather or hapless sports teams. Those all serve to generate a chuckle or two. And none of them serve to slight another individual.

So, in building up your brand and shoring up your status in your professional world, endeavor to make someone laugh.

-72-
Listen For the Next Question

In May 2021, author and personal transformation expert Jeff Nischwitz shared on his daily BED Talk video insight an idea for keeping small talk conversations alive. He calls it listening for the next question.

He shared that in nearly all situations where he is a conversation: "I don't listen for what to say next, how to respond or what advice to give - I literally and fully listen for the next question."

He goes on to elaborate that the power of questions "help people learn, discern, grow and become more self-aware."

There is no special skill to capitalize on this insight. Sure, you must be commitment to it and focused on where your mind it at. But if you intentional practice listening for the next question, in time, will become second nature.

Now, doesn't that sound worthwhile?

-73-
Focus On Their Favorite Topic

According to social architect and networking guru Terry Bean, "Here's the thing about people. Generally, their favorite topic is them. When you are in a networking situation, most people can't wait to tell you what they do and how you can help them. Make it easy on them and make it beneficial for you. Let them. Let them get it all out. Allow them to speak and share what they feel they need to about their business. Pay attention. Ask questions. Listen to answers."

Bean shares this in his book, *Be Connected: Strategies To Attract The Right Opportunities, Connections and Clients Through Effective Networking*. And he goes on to elaborate that this listening is important to build relationships.

Focus on their favorite topic. They will in time want to learn about you. If not, they weren't a good networking prospect anyway. Saving you lots of time.

-74-
Little Help; Long Way

Matt Ward, a consultant to service-based professionals seeking referrals, shared in his book *MORE … Word Of Mouth Referrals, Lifelong Customers and Raving Fan*: "Even though you're crunched for time, I recommend checking in with your contacts on a regular basis and asking how you can help."

Ward goes on to explain that this is simply a matter of reaching out to touch base. They might not even take you up on your offer. But with that offer – if done in a genuine manner – they will know that you care. And when they sense you care, they cannot help but care about you, in kind.

So, this little help you offer, goes a long way to seed the relationships you need to have in your life. And chances are those little seeds you'll have planted will sprout, take root, and provide for you in your time of need.

-75-
Smiles - The Universal Language

In her book *Networking Success: How to Turn Business and Financial Relationships into Fun and Profit*, author Anne Boe, shares, "Smiles are said to be the universal language. A smile is reassuring to the other person and makes you approachable. When two people smile it makes everyone feel good."

Knowing this, you should commit to never embarking out into the world without a big, warm smile. Certainly, there are days where this is easier said than done. But it's never impossible to find a reason to smile. A reason to appreciate all that you have. A reason to love the life you lead.

Because with a smile everyone speaks the same language. And you can communicate love and joy to everyone you see. And when they smile back, they share those feelings with you. Then, together, you make the world a better place.

-76-
Expect Something Wonderful

Industrial revolution businessman and automotive titan Henry Ford once said, "If you think you can or you think you can't, you're usually right." This is somewhat insightful. Maybe, even obvious. It's hard to imagine accomplishing anything worthwhile when deep inside you think you won't.

But beyond the mindset consideration, there is the optics of the situation. You're embarking on something significant, yet your demeanor and effort cannot help but mimic your thoughts.

So, while the world can see you're trying to accomplish something, they can also see that you really aren't giving it your all. Why would you? Afterall, you're bracing for defeat. And that just makes you look mentally weak.

The bottom line is this, in all situations, believe you can. Don't allow doubt to seep into your mind. Sure, believing alone does not guarantee success. But through believing you can expect that something wonderful will come from the experience.

-77-
Sure Things, Wishes, and Dreams

When you were younger, just before your birthday you'd create a list of the things you wanted. Then you'd distribute it to those who cared about you. On that list, were three general categories of items.

One, "sure things." Items that you knew someone would get for you just because they were on the list.

Two, "hopeful wishes." Items you were optimistic about, but you could never quite be sure of receiving.

And, finally, "just dreams." Items that you didn't expect. But maybe … just maybe the star would be properly aligned, and someone would come through.

With your network, everyday should be like your birthday. Always have a list that you communicate. And make sure that list has a mix of sure things, hopeful wishes, and just dreams. People will come through for you. And you just never know when the stars might be properly aligned.

-78-
Curiosity Builds

In his book *MORE: Word of Mouth Referrals, Lifelong Customers and Raving Fans*, word-of-mouth referral consultant Matt Ward shares, "Contrary to the popular saying, curiosity never killed the cat. And it won't kill you. In fact, quite the opposite. Expressing curiosity about your contact's life will open doors you didn't even know existed."

Ward goes on to explain that there is great value in being curious about the lives of the people with whom you associate. Inquiry about pictures they have in their office. Ask where they got that unique piece of jewelry. Be truly curious as to how their weekend was ... how their son is doing at college ... or how their daughter is doing training the new puppy.

As Ward explains, by taking notice and being curious, you build respect and deepen your relationship with your contact. So curiosity doesn't kill. Rather it actually builds.

-79-
The "Successful Networker" Mindset

You likely network for one simple reason: To get. You want others to introduce you to great people who can advance your life. You want your network to alert you to useful ideas and game-changing opportunities.

But to get these things, you need to be open to giving them first. With that in mind, ask yourself these three questions:

1 - Am I willing to "go the extra mile" to help the people around me?

2 - Am I willing to recommend and support the people with whom I associate?

3 - Am I willing to personally rely upon those same people?

To have a successful network, you need to give a resounding "YES" to each of these. After all, if the answer to each and every question is not YES, how could you expect others to rely upon you ... recommend you ... or "go the extra mile" for you?

-80-
Change The Subject

This is the reality: Small talk is the gateway to wonderful relationships. Every great client, vendor, and significant other started with a little chit chat about seemingly something that was basically nothing.

And while small talk is big, everyone struggles to keep a conversation going from time to time. Everyone. A tactic to keep conversations alive and well is to simply change the topic somewhat. That is, you can forever avoid those awkward moments of silence - where no one knows what to say –by just sending the conversation on a fresh new path.

Someone might grow weary of talking about business. Fair enough. Fire up a whole new line of dialogue about their favorite team ... where they've been on vacation ... or about their three great kids. Whatever.

Here's the reality: Conversations don't burn out. It's the subject that runs its course. So, change it. And keep building the relationship.

-81-
The Missing Tile Syndrome

Dennis Prager, an American talk show host, coined the term, "The Missing Tile Syndrome." He asks you to imagine yourself sitting in a room and looking up you notice that a ceiling tile is missing. From then on, no matter how beautiful the ceiling is, you can't fully enjoy it just because of a missing tile.

Then he shifts the conversation to you thinking about your life. Like many people, chances are it's a wonderful one. However, it's not perfect. No one's life is. Other people have things that you don't. Money. Friends. Looks. Careers.

So what? Ignore it. Focus on – and be thankful for – all you have. And chances are you have lots going for you.

As Prager explains, there is a huge problem when you start to focus on the missing tiles in your life. It can make you dissatisfied and rob of the happiness you deserve.

-82-
Act Before Being Asked

Doing something for another in your network is a wonderful gesture. Giving referrals. Making introductions. Sharing information. Any of it, serves to light up someone's world. And that thoughtfulness will likely etch you on their mind forever.

Do you know what would make it even more special? Simple. Act before being asked. Think of it like this: It's well established that you can't tickle yourself. Your brain simply won't allow it, as it knows the contact is coming. Likewise, you enhance the impact of your act of generosity when others don't expect it.

So, think on what others might need. Chances are that their needs for assistance and support are very similar to the things you're looking for.

Once you seize upon something to do, just step up and offer it to them. And as you do delight in their sheer joy of this unexpected moment. No doubt, you'll have made their day.

-83-
When, Not What

As you think about what to say when it's your opportunity share about yourself, remember this: If you're hopeful of empowering others to send you referrals, *what* you do is not nearly as important as *when* you do it.

Here's an example:

If a realtor says they "help people buy and sell houses," they've shared WHAT they do. Unfortunately, this is not as useful in helping to find referrals for them as understanding the WHEN. They help people buy a house WHEN there's a young couple with an infant child in a small apartment. They help people sell a house WHEN a couple's last child moves out to join the grown-up world. And the list could go on.

When are the times WHEN you do what you do? When are the times that you help others? Share those with your network, as that is incredibly useful in helping them identify referrals for you.

-84-
Tell Me About Your Goals

Intuitively it might make sense to sincerely ask the people with whom you network: "How can I assist you in meeting your goals?" After all, effective networking start by adding value to those around you. Don't be surprised, however, If they hesitate to respond in a meaningful way. Why?

First, the question might catch them off guard and they simply might not be ready to articulately answer. Or, they might feel uncomfortable answering, worried that you're somehow judging them. And still, some might hesitate, thinking you're looking for an angle to pitch on something.

A more productive approach might be to explore their goals and objectives first. Certainly, inquire as to where they hope to see things in five years. But also, inquiry as to the challenges facing them over the next five days. They'll likely offer up real answers. And that will give you insight as to how you can help them.

-85-
Harvard Beats Yale 29-29

In 1969, The Yale Bulldogs, with a litany of stars and NFL level talent, was ranked as one of the top teams in college football. And were projected to win the Ivy League title with little competition.

Harvard, on the other hand, was expected to finish last in conference. The media felt it to lacked depth, experience, and star power. Despite this, they were not deterred. They were committed to proving people wrong. And they were not going to concede anything to its Ivy League rival, the much-heralded Yale Bulldogs.

And this mindset paid off. In the season finale against Yale, Harvard scored 16 points in the final 42 seconds to earn a tie as well as secure a share of the Ivy League title. The next day the headline in the Harvard student paper read, "Harvard Beats Yale 29-29."

The lesson is this: Always believe in yourself. And don't buy into the hype of others.

-86-
Jump Out Of Bed

Lifestyle entrepreneur, executive coach, and personal development influencer Lewis Howes shared in his book *The School of Greatness*, "If you don't have a vision that gets you out of bed in the morning, go back to sleep until you find one that does."

While Howes doesn't want you to take that literally, he continues "Your vision is what makes you want to get out of bed. Ultimately though, you have to do it. And you have to do it over and over and over again with every ounce of energy that you have, even on those days when you're suffering the most – especially on those days, in fact."

To be successful, you need to have a powerful reason for doing what you do. It can't be mere money. That won't carry you through the hard times. No, as Howes shares, you need to have a motivation that gets you jumping out of bed.

-87-
Embrace Xenomania

You need people in your life. Everyone does. You might think that somehow, you're the Lone Ranger type and are capable of easily conquer all on your own. Well, stop kidding yourself. No one ... and nothing ... has been created or accomplished by anyone without the assistance of another, somehow.

So, again, you need people in your life. Family. Friends. Community contacts. Employers. Colleagues. Vendors. Even the quiet neighbors that tend to keep to themselves. You need them all.

You also need the people you don't already know. Yes, complete and total strangers are important for building a successful life. These are the people that lead to other wonderful contacts, vital information, and opportunities you didn't know were there.

So, don't shy away from meeting someone new. In fact, take great joy in it. The dictionary definition of this is xenomania – taking pleasure in meeting strangers. Embrace xenomania. Your success depends on it.

-88-
Flow And Stand

Thomas Jefferson, American statesman, Founding Father, and third president of the United States, once remarked "In matters of style, swim with the current; in matters of principle, stand like a rock."

As you know, we live in a time of change on many fronts. To mention a few. Telecommunications. How we shop. Acceptable dress. Means of transportation. On these matters, it's okay to move with the times.

But when it comes to your core principles ... the values that are dearest to you ... such as freedom of thought and expression ... equality for all ... honesty ... appreciation ... these are matter to which your commitment must be steadfast and firm.

When you follow Jefferson's mantra, others know you are principled and disciplined. Through this you strengthen the bonds of trust, which results in committed relationships.

Don't go with the flow when principles are at stake. Rather, stand like a rock and do what is required.

-89-
Relationships Are Gold

Time is money. It's the hours and minutes you devote to an endeavor – coupled with your talents, skills, and experience – that serve to create value for which you can be compensated. And from that, you can have the things you want.

But more valuable than time are the relationships in your life. Family. Friends. Colleagues. Clients. Vendors. And even your competition.

From these relationships you get referrals. And from these opportunities you have something for which you can devote your time. From relationships, you gather information and ideas. And from this insight you can create more value for the time you have to sell. And, finally, from these relationships you are introduced to others. And from these new connections, you increase the potential outlets for your precious and valuable time.

Time will help you have the things you want. But if you want to make the most of this, it's all about the others in your life. Time is money. But relationships are gold.

-90-
Community Crushes Insecurity

Everyone has a level of insecurity. Everyone. It's in the human DNA. We've survived this long because we've been accepted into the community of others to support and care for us. While we really don't live in clans or tribes anymore, the insecurity of not having one lingers on.

So, everybody is insecure. People who seem timid? Insecure. They're just trying to fit in and are uncertain as to how. The gregarious type? Insecure. They appear bold, trying to win favor and be accepted. Everyone in between? Insecure. They also just want just to belong.

You too, likely feel a sense of insecurity. Be honest. Well, here's a secret. A great way to conquer your own insecurity is to help others conquer theirs. Think about it. If we go out of your way to make others feel like they belong, they will want you to be part of their world in return. Together, you've created community. And community crushes insecurity.

-91-
Not Honor, Legacy

No doubt, you'll accomplish much in your life. You'll earn certificates and degrees. You'll rise through the ranks of an organization or corporate life. Perhaps, you'll make a notable contribution of time, talent and treasure within your community. You might even start and build a business empire where employees and clients grow and develop because of you.

Whatever the case, with each and every milestone, what matters most is not the associated individual accolades or honors. Rather, it's the legacy you leave that creates the lasting impact.

Sure, pats on the back are nice. Seeing your name in print will be wonderful. And that plaque will look sharp hanging on your wall. However, each of these will be insignificant in time and will pale in comparison to knowing that what you've done will benefit the future.

It's not the honors you can get that should drive you. Rather, it's the legacy you can leave.

-92-
Be Social on Social Media

History may look back at the innovations of website applications like LinkedIn, Facebook, YouTube, and Twitter as a great liberator of the masses. Never before has seemingly anybody had a voice that has a chance to be heard by everybody.

But as powerful as these mediums are you need to remember that social media is about engaging others. Connecting. Sharing information, thoughts, and opinions. And of course (and this is important), listening.

Social media should never be about denying someone's opinion. It shouldn't be about demeaning or devaluing another. It shouldn't be about pushing out threats or bullying across the electronic ecosystem of the World Wide Web.

The key portion of the term social media is social. This word implies community and relationship building. And those activities require civility. So, to make the best use of social media, attempt to conduct yourself as you would face to face. In short, be social on social media.

-93-
Look To the Overlooked

Wharton School of Business professor Dr. Adam Grant shared on Twitter: "When you only listen to the smartest person in the room, you miss out on discovering what the rest of the room is smart about. Everyone you meet knows something you don't—and has wisdom from experiences you haven't lived. Every conversation is a chance to learn something new."

Grant is right. Everyone can teach you something. And sure, that accomplished person might seem like the best place to get that wonderful nugget of insight that will change your world. You might be surprised at the knowledge and awareness that can come from the person you might otherwise overlook.

You know that person who might not seem quite as accomplished. Or, that person who is never really front and center. And even, that quiet person who is carefully listening and taking in everything that others have to say. If you want insight, look to those who others might overlook.

-94-
Subsequent Impressions

Social architect Terry Bean shared in his book Be *Connected: Strategies To Attract The Right Opportunities, Connections And Clients Through Effective Networking*: "You've no doubt been taught and believe the idea that you never get a second chance to make a first impression. While technically true, I don't believe it matters."

Bean goes on to indicate that often people make a great impression at first and then disappoint later. Or vice versa. But moreover, feeling that you have this one and only chance to make this initial impression you try too hard to WOW them. And in so doing, you totally miss the opportunity to learn about them.

What's Bean's strategy? Start all your conversations by inviting them to go first. Something like: "What inspired you to get into this profession?"

In short, discover who they are and rely on subsequent encounters to share about you. They will be duly impressed.

-95-
Build Alliances

In his book *The 40 Laws of Networking*, global connector, Germaine Moody establishes as law number six, "Build Alliances" He shares: "Connecting with the right people, organizations and businesses in the right regions, industries, and sectors, at the right time is absolutely crucial to your influence."

Moody's insight alludes to the notion that you do nothing alone. All of your success comes from the people around you. These are alliances. And they are a surefire way to increase your credibility, which in turn builds your influence.

Moody goes on to remark that alliance serve to cover your back ... make you appear larger or smarter than you are ... they can help you persuade the emotions and decisions of others ... and they can create immeasurable access to even more alliances.

Alliances! Making creating them your endgame. And then those alliances will serve as the beginning of great things.

-96-
A Galvanizing Event

You look to achieve. You can clearly see it in your mind. And you diligently work hard to make it happen. Despite all of this, however, sometimes things don't always work out as you might hope. And that hurts. This disappointment, however, can be a galvanizing event - if you let it.

When you meet with such a setback, stand tall, face into it, and take it in. Don't allow the moment to sour you on life. Rather, let the experience toughen your resolve. Allow the moment to teach you something. Allow it to forge you into a better person. Allow it to drive you forward towards another objective.

Sure, disappointment is never fun. But if you commit to growing from it, you'll be better prepared to take on the next challenge. And the reality is that another challenge is coming. So you're best to rise above your disappointment and move on.

-97-
Hope From the Past

Winston Churchill, best known for his wartime leadership as Prime Minister of Great Britain during the Second World War, once remarked: "The future is unknowable, but the past should give us hope."

There is nothing insightful about asserting that no one can predict the future. Many have tried. And most have been wrong in one form or another. But deriving hope from the past is a powerful notion.

You simply have no idea as to how your life will unfold from this point forward. Future relationships. Career. Business. It's all unknowable, as Churchill states.

But, as many great businesses and careers have started exactly where you're at, you should be optimistic. Likewise, as the past has many examples of first meetings blossoming into great relationships, you should be excited about those new acquaintances. Look around. The accomplishments of others are windows to a time gone by. These past lives should give you hope for your future.

-98-
The Four-Step Loop

According to Brian Ahearn, author of Influence PEOPLE: Powerful Everyday Opportunities to Persuade that are Lasting and Ethical, a good reciprocal relationship is one where there is a willingness to give and receive. He illustrates this by having people envision a four-step loop.

The first step is that you must have both the ability and a sincere desire to help to others. Beyond that, the second step of the loop is that those people need to be open to accepting your generosity – whatever it might be.

But beyond receiving from you, for the loop to continue these people must empower the third step by having a genuine desire to reciprocate to you. And finally, for the fourth step, you need to be willing to receive their efforts to reciprocate.

Each of these steps is vital to creating a solid long-term relationship. So, know what you can give to others, but also know what you need in return.

-99-
The Approachable Person

When you're out networking, the objective is to build relationships with others. To accomplish this, you need to engage in conversations. Whether you talk about the big game, the weather, or the quality of the coffee in your hand is not really important. It's simple a matter of engaging in small talk.

As you venture into that next event, however, heed the advice of Debra Fine, author of The Fine Art Of Small Talk: "It is much easier to engage one person than enter a group conversation, so begin by looking for the "approachable" person. HINT: This person is the one who makes eye contact and is not actively engaged in conversation with anyone else."

Fine is right. It's simply awkward inserting yourself into an ongoing conversation. But at any outing, there is someone standing or sitting alone. That is the person you need to approach and say little more than, "What do you think of this coffee?"

-100-
Moment of Doubt

Think of that great movie. You know, the one where it feels like the bad guys might actually win. Or the flix where the relationship you're rooting for seems like it just might never be. Then through perseverance, creativity and perhaps a dash of luck, the ending you hope for falls into place. What a great feeling.

Sure, that's Hollywood doing its magic. But that's life too. You see, to achieve amazing success there is generally that point. That point where things are incredibly challenging. That patch of time where the world seems to be conspiring against you. That moment where it feels like the bad guys – you know the doubters, detractors, and naysayers in your life – might actually win.

You know what? These trials are not a bad thing. In fact, they're necessary. Thinks about it. If you don't experience these moments of doubt, just like the movies, the happy ending will not be as happy as it could be.

-101-
The Biggest Benefit of Knowing

Social architect Terry Bean encourages in his book Be Connected that you should take time to really understand others – who they are and how you can be of service to them. Simple, right?

According to Bean, the biggest benefit of getting to know others is that you will be able to remember their name. Yes, remember their name. And that's important. After all, you can't remember something you never knew. As Bean states, "We are so busy trying to "impress" people when we first meet them that we rarely hear their name when we are introduced."

Bean's strategy flips that script. Dial into who they are, what they do, and how you might serve them. And with that you'll naturally be more likely to remember their name.

And then, without saying much at all, you'll become incredibly impressive in their eyes. And from that, they will want to remember your name too.

There you have it—101 essays. But we wanted to offer a bonus essay. Before we do, if you're interested in exploring other books, content, and programs by Frank Agin, visit frankagin.com or simply search "Frank Agin" on whatever platform you use to get great content.

-102-
It's What You Do

It's often said that "It's not what you know, but who you know." And that's true. It really is. Think about it. All the knowledge in the world is worthless without someone to share it with.

So, it's not what you know, but who you know. Well … sort of. It is possible to know lots of people – wonderfully, influential people – and be no better off than someone who doesn't. For example, you might know that wonderful someone and they want nothing to do with you.

So, knowing people is not enough. To benefit from the people you know, they also need to like and trust you. It's this like and trust coupled with people knowing you that is the foundation upon which relationships are formed.

So, it's not what you know. Nor it is who you know. Rather it's what you do to build relationships that matters the most.

About The Author

Frank Agin is president of AmSpirit Business Connections, which empowers entrepreneurs, sales representatives, and professionals to become successful and gain more referrals through networking.

He also shares information and insights on professional relationships, business networking and best practices for generating referrals on his Networking Rx podcast and through various professional programs.

Finally, Frank is the author of several books, including *Foundational Networking: Building Know, Like & Trust to Create a Life of Extraordinary Success*. See all his books and programs at frankagin.com. You can reach him at frankagin@amspirit.com.